Animals in the Wild

Gorilla

by Mary Hoffman

Raintree Childrens Books
Milwaukee • Toronto • Melbourne • London
Belitha Press Limited • London

Mountain gorillas live in Africa. So do
lowland gorillas. Gorillas belong to the ape
family. Other apes are orangutans,
chimpanzees, and gibbons.

Baby gorillas are born one at a time. They weigh over four pounds. When the mothers travel, the babies hang onto their mothers' bellies.

Mothers spend all of their time with their babies, feeding and grooming them.

Gorillas live in groups that have at least
one male, several females, and young.

All of the males of the group allow the babies to play. A fully grown male gorilla is called a silverback.

When males are about fifteen years old,
their fur turns silver-gray. Males weigh over
300 pounds.

Gorillas usually walk on all fours. They stand five feet tall. The oldest silverback is the leader who looks after his family.

Younger males help to keep watch and sound the alarm if there is any danger.

Mountain gorillas live on volcanoes in Africa. Plants that the gorillas like to eat grow in the rain forests there.

Gorillas are vegetarians. They eat leaves and berries and juicy shoots. They climb well, especially for food.

It rains hard in the rain forests. Gorillas
huddle in trees in the rain.

Gorillas build nests to sleep in, both day and night. The nests are untidy.

Silverbacks will defend their families to the death. But if the leader is killed, the group might split up.

Only humans and other gorillas attack gorillas. People have killed all but a few hundred mountain gorillas.

Some people have tried to help the gorillas. John Aspinall started a gorilla group in a zoo park in England. Gorillas are very peaceful animals. They seem to like people.

Dian Fossey lived with mountain gorillas
for thirteen years. They became good
friends. She helped to stop poachers from
killing them. The gorillas need to be
protected in order to survive.

First published in this edition in the United States of America 1985
by Raintree Publishers Inc., 330 East Kilbourn Avenue,
Milwaukee, Wisconsin 53202.

First published in the United Kingdom under the title
Animals in the Wild—Gorilla
by Belitha Press Ltd.,
2 Beresford Terrace, London N5 2DH
in association with Methuen Children's Books Ltd.

Library of Congress Number: 84-24906

Dedicated to Nicholas, Tom, and Stephen.

Scientific Adviser: Dr. Gwynne Vevers. Picture Researcher: Stella Martin

Acknowledgements are due to Bob Campbell for all photographs in this book
with the following exceptions: Survival Anglia pp. 2, 10 and 15; Natural
Science Photos pp. 5, 8 and 16; Bruce Coleman Ltd p. 11; Howletts Zoo
Parks, Nr Canterbury, Kent p. 22. Front cover: Photograph by Bob Campbell.
Back Cover: Natural Science Photos.

Special Acknowledgement
All pictures of gorillas in this book, except that on p. 22, are of mountain
gorillas. Many of these were taken at Dian Fossey's Karisoke Research Centre
in Rwanda and we should like to acknowledge her pioneering work with the mountain gorilla.

ISBN 0-8172-2413-0 (U.S.A.)

Library of Congress Cataloging in Publication Data

Hoffman, Mary
  Gorilla.

  (Animals in the wild)
  Summary: Depicts the gorilla in its natural surroundings
and describes its life and sturggles for survival.
    1. Gorillas—Juvenile literature. (1. Gorillas) I. Title. II. Series.
QL737.P96S48 1985   599.88'46   84-24906

1 2 3 4 5 6 7 8 9   89 88 87 86 85